D0094465

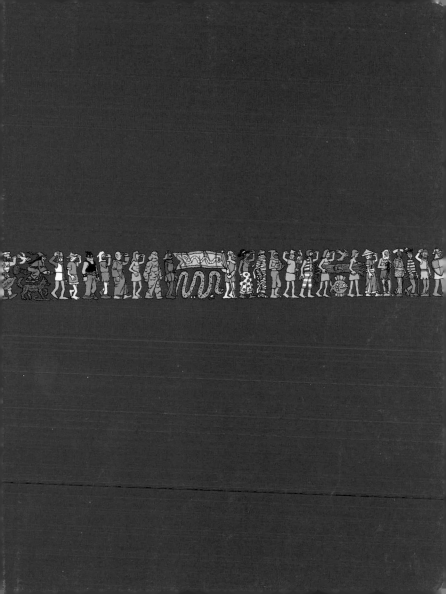

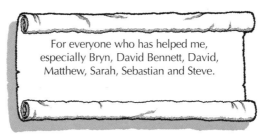

For everyone who has helped me,
especially Bryn, David Bennett, David,
Matthew, Sarah, Sebastian and Steve.

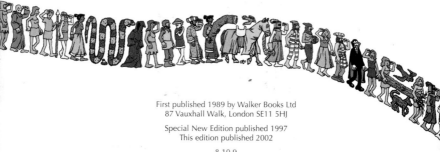

First published 1989 by Walker Books Ltd
87 Vauxhall Walk, London SE11 5HJ

Special New Edition published 1997
This edition published 2002

8 10 9

© 1989, 1995, 1997 Martin Handford

The right of Martin Handford to be identified as author/illustrator
of this work has been asserted by him in accordance with the
Copyright, Designs and Patents Act 1988

Printed in China

British Library Cataloguing in Publication Data:
a catalogue record for this book
is available from the British Library

ISBN-13: 978-0-7445-9445-4
ISBN-10: 0-7445-9445-6

www.walkerbooks.co.uk

WHERE'S WALLY? ③ THE FANTASTIC JOURNEY

MARTIN HANDFORD

WALKER BOOKS
AND SUBSIDIARIES
LONDON · BOSTON · SYDNEY · AUCKLAND

THE GOBBLING GLUTTONS

ONCE UPON A TIME WALLY
EMBARKED UPON A FANTASTIC
JOURNEY. FIRST, AMONG A
THRONG OF GOBBLING GLUTTONS,
HE MET WIZARD WHITEBEARD, WHO
COMMANDED HIM TO FIND A SCROLL AND
THEN TO FIND ANOTHER AT EVERY STAGE OF
HIS JOURNEY. FOR WHEN HE HAD FOUND
12 SCROLLS, HE WOULD UNDERSTAND THE
TRUTH ABOUT HIMSELF.

IN EVERY PICTURE FIND WALLY, WOOF (BUT ALL
YOU CAN SEE IS HIS TAIL), WENDA, WIZARD
WHITEBEARD, ODLAW AND THE SCROLL. THEN
FIND WALLY'S KEY, WOOF'S BONE (IN THIS SCENE
IT'S THE BONE THAT'S NEAREST TO HIS TAIL),
WENDA'S CAMERA AND ODLAW'S BINOCULARS.

THERE ARE ALSO 25 WALLY-WATCHERS, EACH OF
WHOM APPEARS ONLY ONCE SOMEWHERE IN
THE FOLLOWING 12 PICTURES. AND ONE MORE
THING! CAN YOU FIND ANOTHER CHARACTER,
NOT SHOWN BELOW, WHO APPEARS ONCE IN
EVERY PICTURE EXCEPT THE LAST?

THE BATTLING MONKS

THEN WALLY AND WIZARD WHITEBEARD CAME
TO THE PLACE WHERE THE INVISIBLE MONKS
OF FIRE FOUGHT THE MONKS OF WATER. AND
AS WALLY SEARCHED FOR THE SECOND SCROLL,
HE SAW THAT MANY WALLIES HAD BEEN THIS WAY BEFORE.
AND WHEN HE FOUND THE SCROLL, IT WAS TIME TO
CONTINUE WITH HIS JOURNEY.

THE CARPET FLYERS

THEN WALLY AND WIZARD WHITEBEARD CAME
TO THE LAND OF THE CARPET FLYERS, WHERE
MANY WALLIES HAD BEEN BEFORE. AND
WALLY SAW THAT THERE WERE MANY
CARPETS IN THE SKY AND MANY RED BIRDS
(HOW MANY, OH BRAINY BIRD AND CARPET WATCHERS?).
AND WHEN WALLY FOUND THE THIRD SCROLL, IT WAS
TIME TO CONTINUE WITH HIS JOURNEY.

THE GREAT BALL-GAME PLAYERS

THEN WALLY AND WIZARD WHITEBEARD CAME TO
THE PLAYING FIELD OF THE GREAT BALL-GAME
PLAYERS, WHERE MANY WALLIES HAD BEEN BEFORE.
AND WALLY SAW THAT FOUR TEAMS WERE PLAYING AGAINST
EACH OTHER (BUT WAS ANYONE WINNING? WHAT WAS THE
SCORE? CAN YOU WORK OUT THE RULES?). THEN WALLY FOUND
THE FOURTH SCROLL AND CONTINUED WITH HIS JOURNEY.

THE FEROCIOUS RED DWARVES

THEN WALLY AND WIZARD WHITEBEARD CAME
AMONG THE FEROCIOUS RED DWARVES, WHERE
MANY WALLIES HAD BEEN BEFORE. AND THE
DWARVES WERE ATTACKING THE MANY-COLOURED
SPEARMEN, CAUSING MIGHTY MAYHEM AND HORRID
HAVOC. AND WALLY FOUND THE FIFTH SCROLL, AND
CONTINUED WITH HIS JOURNEY.

THE NASTY NASTIES

THEN WALLY AND WIZARD WHITEBEARD CAME TO
THE CASTLE OF THE NASTY NASTIES, WHERE
MANY WALLIES HAD BEEN BEFORE. AND
WHEREVER WALLY WALKED, THERE WAS A CLATTERING
OF BONES (WOOF'S BONE IN THIS SCENE IS THE NEAREST TO
HIS TAIL) AND A FOUL SLURPING OF FILTHY FOOD. AND WALLY
FOUND THE SIXTH SCROLL AND CONTINUED WITH HIS JOURNEY.

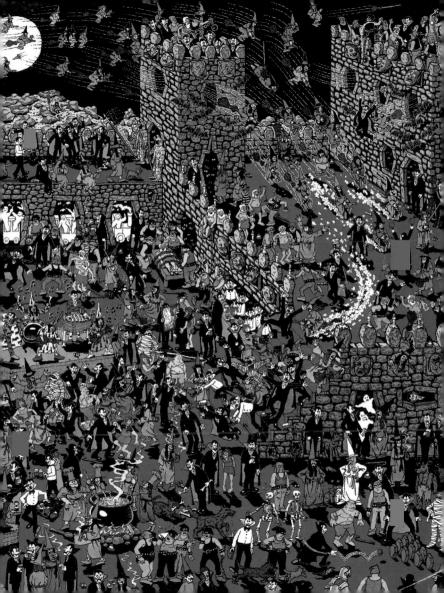

THE FIGHTING FORESTERS

THEN WALLY AND WIZARD WHITEBEARD CAME AMONG THE FIGHTING FORESTERS, WHERE MANY WALLIES HAD BEEN BEFORE. AND IN THEIR BATTLE WITH THE EVIL BLACK KNIGHTS, THE FOREST WOMEN WERE AIDED BY THE ANIMALS, BY THE LIVING MUD, EVEN BY THE TREES THEMSELVES. AND WALLY FOUND THE SEVENTH SCROLL AND CONTINUED WITH HIS JOURNEY.

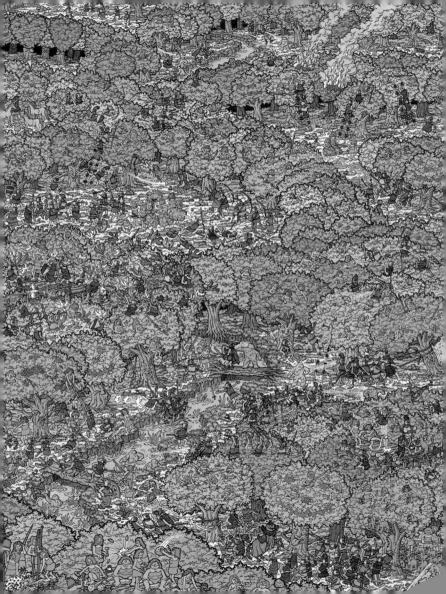

THE DEEP-SEA DIVERS

THEN WALLY AND WIZARD WHITEBEARD CAME TO
THE WATERY WORLD OF THE DEEP-SEA DIVERS,
WHERE MANY WALLIES HAD BEEN BEFORE. AND
WALLY SEARCHED FOR THE EIGHTH SCROLL AMONG
THE MONSTERS OF THE DEEP, AMONG THE MERMAIDS,
FISHERMEN AND FISH. AND WHEN HE FOUND IT, IT WAS TIME
TO CONTINUE WITH HIS JOURNEY.

THE KNIGHTS OF THE MAGIC FLAG

THEN WALLY AND WIZARD WHITEBEARD CAME
TO A PLACE MORE CROWDED THAN ANY WALLY
HAD SEEN BEFORE, WHERE TWO ARMIES WITH
MANY MAGIC FLAGS WERE LOCKED IN COMBAT.
AND WALLY SAW THAT MANY WALLIES HAD BEEN THIS WAY
BEFORE. AND WHEN HE FOUND THE NINTH SCROLL, IT WAS
TIME TO CONTINUE WITH HIS JOURNEY.

THE UNFRIENDLY GIANTS

THEN WALLY AND WIZARD WHITEBEARD CAME TO
THE LAND OF THE UNFRIENDLY GIANTS, WHERE
MANY WALLIES HAD BEEN BEFORE. AND WALLY
SAW THAT THE GIANTS WERE HORRIDLY
HARASSING THE LITTLE PEOPLE. AND WHEN HE FOUND THE
TENTH SCROLL, IT WAS TIME TO CONTINUE WITH HIS JOURNEY.

THE UNDERGROUND HUNTERS

THEN WALLY AND WIZARD WHITEBEARD CAME
AMONG THE UNDERGROUND HUNTERS, WHERE
MANY WALLIES HAD BEEN BEFORE. AND THERE
WAS MUCH MENACE IN THIS PLACE, AND A
MULTITUDE OF MALEVOLENT MONSTERS. AND
WALLY FOUND THE ELEVENTH SCROLL AND CONTINUED
WITH HIS JOURNEY.

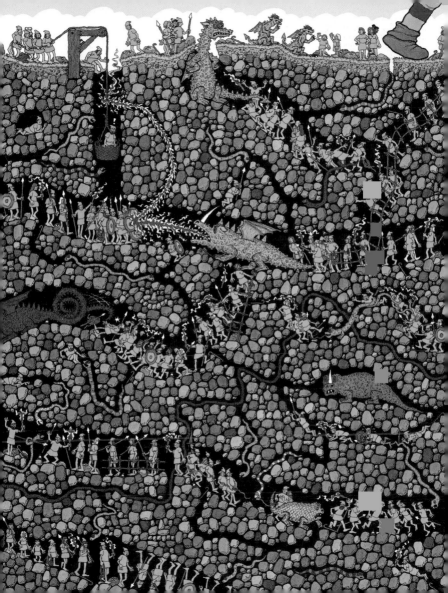

THE LAND OF WALLIES

THEN WALLY FOUND THE TWELFTH SCROLL AND SAW THE
TRUTH ABOUT HIMSELF, THAT HE WAS JUST ONE WALLY
AMONG MANY. HE SAW TOO THAT WALLIES OFTEN LOSE
THINGS, FOR HE HIMSELF HAD LOST ONE SHOE. AND AS
HE LOOKED FOR HIS SHOE, HE DISCOVERED THAT WIZARD
WHITEBEARD WAS NOT HIS ONLY FELLOW TRAVELLER. THERE WERE NOW
ELEVEN OTHERS - ONE FROM EVERY PLACE HE HAD BEEN TO -
WHO HAD JOINED HIM ONE BY ONE ALONG THE WAY. SO NOW (OH LOYAL
FOLLOWERS OF WALLY!) FIND THE REAL WALLY AND HELP HIM FIND HIS
MISSING SHOE. AND THERE, IN THE LAND OF WALLIES,
MAY WALLY LIVE HAPPILY EVER AFTER.

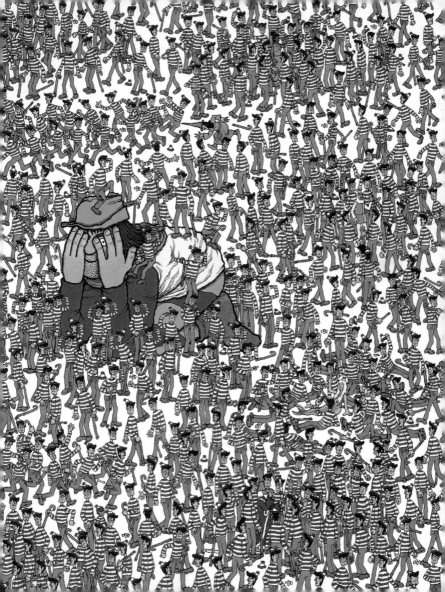

THE GOBBLING GLUTTONS

- [ ] A strong waiter and a weak one
- [ ] Long-distance smells
- [ ] Unequal portions of pie
- [ ] A man who has had too much to drink
- [ ] People who are going the wrong way
- [ ] Very tough dishes
- [ ] An upside-down dish
- [ ] A very hot dinner
- [ ] Knights drinking through straws
- [ ] A clever drink-pourer
- [ ] Giant sausages
- [ ] A custard fight
- [ ] An overloaded seat
- [ ] Beard-flavoured soup
- [ ] Men pulling legs
- [ ] A painful spillage
- [ ] A poke in the eye
- [ ] A man tied up in spaghetti
- [ ] A knock-out dish
- [ ] A man who has eaten too much
- [ ] A tall diner eating a tall dish
- [ ] An exploding pie
- [ ] A giant sausage breaking in half
- [ ] A smell travelling through two people

THE CARPET FLYERS

- [ ] Two carpets on collision course
- [ ] An overweight flyer
- [ ] A pedestrian crossing
- [ ] A carpet pin-up
- [ ] Three hangers-on
- [ ] Flying hitch-hikers
- [ ] An unsatisfied customer
- [ ] A used carpet salesman
- [ ] A topsy-turvy tower
- [ ] A spiky crash
- [ ] Carpet cops and robbers
- [ ] A passing fruit thief
- [ ] Upside-down flyers
- [ ] A carpet repair shop
- [ ] Popular male and female flyers
- [ ] A flying tower
- [ ] A stair carpet
- [ ] Flying highwaymen
- [ ] Rich and poor flyers
- [ ] A carpet-breakdown rescue service
- [ ] Carpets flying on carpet flyers
- [ ] A carpet traffic policeman
- [ ] A flying carpet without a flyer

THE BATTLING MONKS

- [ ] Two fire engines
- [ ] Hot-footed monks
- [ ] A bridge made of monks
- [ ] A cheeky monk
- [ ] A diving monk
- [ ] A scared statue
- [ ] Fire meeting water
- [ ] A snaking jet of water
- [ ] Chasers being chased
- [ ] A smug statue
- [ ] A snaking jet of flame
- [ ] A five-way wash-out
- [ ] A burning bridge
- [ ] Seven burning backsides
- [ ] Monks worshipping the Flowing Bucket of Water
- [ ] Monks shielding themselves from lava
- [ ] Thirteen trapped and extremely worried monks
- [ ] A monk seeing an oncoming jet of flame
- [ ] Monks worshipping the Mighty Erupting Volcano
- [ ] A very worried monk confronted by two opponents
- [ ] A burning hose
- [ ] Monks and lava pouring out of a volcano
- [ ] A chain of water
- [ ] Two monks accidentally attacking their brothers

THE GREAT BALL-GAME PLAYERS

- [ ] A three-way drink
- [ ] A row of hand-held banners
- [ ] A chase that goes round in circles
- [ ] A spectator surrounded by three rival supporters
- [ ] Players who can't see where they are going
- [ ] Two tall players versus short ones
- [ ] Seven awful singers
- [ ] A face made of balls
- [ ] Players who are digging for victory
- [ ] A face about to hit a fist
- [ ] A shot that breaks the woodwork
- [ ] A mob chasing a player backwards
- [ ] A player chasing a mob
- [ ] Players pulling each other's hoods
- [ ] A flag with a hole in it
- [ ] A mob of players all holding balls
- [ ] A player heading a ball
- [ ] A player tripping over a rock
- [ ] A player punching a ball
- [ ] A spectator accidentally hitting two others
- [ ] A player poking his tongue out at a mob
- [ ] A mouth pulled open by a beard
- [ ] A backside shot

THE FEROCIOUS RED DWARVES

- [ ] A spear-breaking slingshot
- [ ] Two punches causing chain reactions
- [ ] Fat and thin spears and spearmen
- [ ] A spearman being knocked through a flag
- [ ] A collar made out of a shield
- [ ] A prison made of spears
- [ ] Tangled spears
- [ ] A devious disarmer
- [ ] Dwarves disguised as spearmen
- [ ] A stick-up machine
- [ ] A spearman trapped by his battle dress
- [ ] A sneaky spear-bender
- [ ] An axe-head causing headaches
- [ ] A dwarf who is on the wrong side
- [ ] Cheeky target practice
- [ ] Opponents charging through each other
- [ ] A spearman running away from a spear
- [ ] A slingshot causing a chain reaction
- [ ] A sword cutting through a shield
- [ ] A spear hitting a spearman's shield
- [ ] A dwarf hiding up a spear
- [ ] Spearmen who have jumped out of their clothes
- [ ] A spear knocking off a dwarf's helmet

THE NASTY NASTIES

- [ ] A vampire who is scared of ghosts
- [ ] Two vampire bears
- [ ] Vampires drinking through straws
- [ ] Gargoyle lovers
- [ ] An upside-down torture
- [ ] A baseball bat
- [ ] Three wolfmen
- [ ] A mummy who is coming undone
- [ ] A vampire mirror test
- [ ] A frightened skeleton
- [ ] Dog, cat and mouse doorways
- [ ] Courting cats
- [ ] A ghoulish game of skittles
- [ ] A gargoyle being poked in the eye
- [ ] An upside-down gargoyle
- [ ] Ghoulish flight controllers
- [ ] Three witches flying backwards
- [ ] A witch losing her broomstick
- [ ] A broomstick flying a witch
- [ ] A ticklish torture
- [ ] A vampire about to get the chop
- [ ] A ghost train
- [ ] A vampire who doesn't fit his coffin
- [ ] A three-eyed, hooded torturer

THE FIGHTING FORESTERS
- Three long legs
- A three-legged knight
- Knights being chopped down by a tree
- Two multiple knock-outs
- A lazy lady
- A tree with a lot of puff
- Hard-headed women
- Attackers about to be attacked
- A strong woman and a weak one
- An easily frightened horse
- Eight pairs of upside-down feet
- Knights shooting arrows at knights
- An upside-down ladder
- Loving trees
- An upside-down trunk
- A two-headed unicorn
- A unicorn in a tree
- Trees with two faces
- Muddy mud-slingers
- A tearful small tree
- Spears getting sharpened tips
- Trees branching out violently
- Stilts being chewed up

THE KNIGHTS OF THE MAGIC FLAG
- Unfaithful royals
- A flag full of fists
- A game of noughts and crosses
- A sword-fighting reindeer
- A man behind bars
- A mouse among lions
- Flags within a flag
- A tangle of tongues
- A zebra crossing
- An eagle dropping an eyeful
- A puffing spoilsport
- A battering-ram door key
- Snakes and ladders
- A flame-throwing dragon
- Diminishing puddings
- A crown thief
- A thirsty lion
- A weapon's imbalance
- A foot being tickled by a feather
- Some cheeky soldiers
- A surrendering reindeer
- A dog straining to get a bone
- A helmet with three eyes

THE DEEP-SEA DIVERS
- A two-headed fish
- A sword fight with a swordfish
- Fish fingers
- A sea bed
- A fish face
- A catfish and a dogfish
- A jellyfish
- A fish with two tails
- A skate
- A sea-lion
- Two fish-shaped formations
- Treacherous treasure
- Oyster-beds
- Tinned fish
- Flying fish
- Electric eels
- A deck of cards
- A bottle in a message
- A fake fin
- A back to front mermaid
- A seahorse-drawn carriage
- A boat's compass
- A fish catching men
- An underwater beach scene
- Divers drawing on an angry sea monster

THE LAND OF WALLIES
- Wallies waving
- Wallies walking
- Wallies running
- Wallies sitting
- Wallies lying down
- Wallies sliding
- Wallies standing still
- Wallies smiling
- Wallies searching
- Wallies being chased
- Wallies giving the thumbs-up
- Wallies looking frightened
- Wallies with bobble hats
- Wallies without bobble hats
- Wallies raising their bobble hats
- Wallies with walking sticks
- Wallies without walking sticks
- Wallies with spectacles
- Wallies without spectacles
- A Wally on a hat
- A Wally holding a wing
- Wally

THE UNDERGROUND HUNTERS
- A hunter about to put his foot in it
- Four frightened flames
- A snaky hat thief
- An underground traffic policeman
- Three surrendering flames
- A two-headed snake
- A snaky tickle
- A ridiculously long snake
- Three dragons wearing sunglasses
- A dragon that attacks with both ends
- Angry snake-parents
- Five broken spears
- A monstrous bridge
- Five rock faces
- Upside-down hunters
- A snake that is trapped
- A very long ladder
- A torch setting fire to spears
- Hunters tripped by a tongue
- A hunter with an extra long spear
- Hunters about to collide
- Hunters going round in a circle
- A shocked tail-puller

THE UNFRIENDLY GIANTS
- Trappers about to be trapped
- A catapulted missile hitting people
- A hairy bird's nest
- Ducks out of water
- A morking giant about to come unstuck
- Two broom trees
- Two giants who are out for the count
- Two windmill knock-outs
- A polite giant about to get a headache
- A giant with a roof over his head
- Three people in a giant hood
- A battering-fist
- A house shaker
- A drawing-pin trap
- A landslide of boulders
- Six people strapped inside giant belts
- People taking part in a beard game
- People being swept off their feet
- Rope-pullers being pulled
- Birds being disturbed by a giant
- Two game-watchers slapping people
- Four shy ladies being flattered
- A powerful burst of pond water

THE FANTASTIC JOURNEY
Did you find Wally, his friends and all the things which they had lost? Did you find the mystery character who appeared in every scene except the land of Wallies? It may be difficult, but keep searching and eventually you'll find him – now that's a clue! And one last thing: somewhere one of the Wally-watchers lost the bobble from his hat. Can you spot which one, and find the bobble?